Welsh oak high
dresser, c. 1760

Pine dresser, c. 1820

Small painted dresser,
early 20th century

Large Huon pine dresser,
19th century

Small Huon
pine dresser,
19th century

Large Edwardian painted
dresser, late 19th or early
20th century

Barossa Valley
painted dresser
with glazed doors,
early 20th century

Barossa Valley
dresser with
original paint,
late 19th century

Dresser with
zinc-mesh
food-safe base,
19th century

Elm-and-oak dresser,
c. 18th century

Pine dresser,
19th century

Pine dresser, 19th century

Dresser with
glazed doors,
early 20th
century

Painted farm dresser
with homespun
metal repairs,
19th century

Tasmanian
dresser, c. 1910

Australian-made
dresser with
original paint,
early 20th century

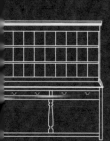

Welsh oak dresser,
18th century

French pine dresser,
18th century

French oak dresser,
18th century

Tasmanian Huon
pine dresser

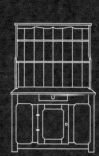

Tasmanian Huon
pine dresser

# THE
# KITCHEN DRESSER

TO MUM AND DAD

# THE
# KITCHEN DRESSER

## IN PRAISE OF
## A FURNITURE ICON

SIMON GRIFFITHS

T&H

# CONTENTS

# FOREWORD

An antique or vintage dresser, whether it be inherited or bought, provides a link to the past. It is usually a treasured possession that has been passed down through generations of previous owners.

This book presents us with many examples of Australian, British and European dressers; some may have been brought to Australia by immigrants from Britain and Europe, and others have been imported later. It is heartwarming to see many fine examples from our home country of Wales being loved and displayed so beautifully. It is also fascinating to see so many examples of dressers constructed in Australia, some in styles we would identify as Welsh, Irish or English and others that have an original Australian style.

In the decades or centuries since many of these dressers were built, the role of the kitchen within our homes has changed. It is no longer the place where we just cook, prepare and eat food: for many of us it is also the place where we meet as a family, work and entertain friends. It is the heart of the home, used all day, every day. In the homes photographed for this book, it is fitting to see how the dresser consciously dominates and is often the focal point of the room. Unlike the kitchen cupboard, which hides its contents behind solid doors, the dresser bares its contents for all to see. It is a piece of furniture that exposes its owner's style and individuality.

The kitchen dresser is a place to display treasured possessions – the prized collection of blue-and-white ceramics, pewter or treen, perhaps an 18th-century plate, baskets and kitchenalia, pottery hens, Staffordshire figures, a brightly coloured collection of Bosley Pottery or everyday modern mugs or bowls. The more diverse its contents, the better it can look. However, not only is the dresser the home of the aesthetically pleasing or valuable, it is also the place where the transient but important things of life may be casually left or displayed – a birthday card that made us laugh, a child's picture, the car keys or even a vaccination certificate.

In this book, Simon Griffiths has gathered a diverse group of dressers. Whether made from Welsh oak, English elm or Tasmanian Huon pine, they are all handcrafted and exhibit their own beauty. This book sings the praises of this furniture icon. Long may the kitchen dresser be used and cherished and remain at the heart of our home.

**Tim and Betsan Bowen**
Authors of *The Welsh Stick Chair: A Visual Record*

Carmarthenshire, West Wales

OPPOSITE
*Part of James Broadbent's enviable collection of early salt-glaze ceramics, pewter and a beautiful early blue-and-white cow-jug creamer (page 173).*

# INTRODUCTION

*The Kitchen Dresser* is a book about the humble dresser. It celebrates what people do with their dressers and how they display objects on them. A dresser groaning with objects instantly gives a house some soul and a feeling of history. Some people prefer their dresser to have a formal appearance, displaying a collection of one type or colour of china, for example, but I think a dresser develops its own personality when it is allowed to accumulate bits and bobs. I grew up with one that Mum and Dad had built by a craftsman in the 1970s, so I have a great love for dressers.

Traditionally a dresser was placed against a wall in a farmhouse or cottage kitchen and was where meat and other food were prepared and dressed for the table – hence the name 'dresser'. It might be called a kitchen dresser, a china hutch or a Welsh dresser, depending on where you are in the world.

The original dresser was just the base, but as time went on, makers added shelves, drawers and sometimes cupboards. There were lots of variations: a plate rack was optional; a dresser might have a high or a low top (these are called high and low dressers, respectively); there might be a potboard at the bottom for heavy cooking pots; the shelves might or might not have backboards; and some dressers were just a base. Dressers varied locally, too. For example, a Scottish dresser might have a tin-lined drawer into which the weekly batch of porridge was poured; pieces of porridge would then be cut from the drawer for eating. Irish dressers were made all in one piece, while English and Welsh dressers were made in two pieces: if the base and the plate rack were separate pieces, it was easier to get them into a small cottage and then slot them together.

Over the years the utilitarian nature of the dresser changed, and it began to be used to display the owner's best china, silver, pewter and other wares. Decorative friezes and ornamentation were added to elevate the quality of the dresser. As such, it was often shifted out of the kitchen and into the dining room as an object of status.

Collectors are great fans of the dresser, as it makes an ideal place to exhibit whatever they collect – antique china, Staffordshire dogs, ceramic jelly moulds, majolica pottery, antique Chinese export porcelain, even opportunity-shop china. Just about anything looks good on a dresser. With most collectors there is a story attached to each item and a preferred way to display their treasures. Meeting collectors and being given a personal tour of their private kingdoms is one of the best parts of my job. It doesn't matter what they collect – paperweights, colonial timber boxes, china figures – I always learn a lot and see rare and wonderful things.

OPPOSITE
*Handcrafted pine dresser with leadlight doors, 1970s*

For many of the dressers in this book, there is no accurate date for when they were made. It is relatively easy to date the English and Welsh dressers, but a lot of those made in Australia were constructed by early-colonial settlers with whatever they had at hand, such as bits of packing cases and leftover wood from goodness knows where – the little Mirka Mora dresser on page 160 is a good example of this. Identifying the date of a piece by its style can be misleading, too, as it took time for new looks and styles to filter out to the colonies.

Identifying the timber used for dressers made in Australia is equally difficult. Oak, elm, pine and some Australian timbers, such as Huon pine and Australian cedar, are fairly easy to identify, but a lot of local timbers look so similar when milled and finished that it's impossible to know what they are.

The dressers in this book reveal many forms: traditional, rustic, pine, oak, painted, as well as new interpretations of the well-loved classics. Whether you have a museum-quality Welsh oak dresser, a pine dresser or a modern version, there is one for every budget and infinite ways to arrange and display items on it.

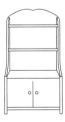

RIGHT

*Child's green dresser, 20th century*

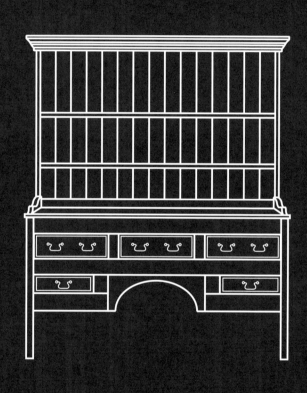

# KITCHEN
# DRESSERS

# THE DRESSER AT MEADOWBANK

---

## SIMON GRIFFITHS

Walking past the dresser in our cottage, Meadowbank, you hear the gentle rattle of china. Jugs and mugs fill the original hooks and the slightest movement in the old floor sets them gently swinging. The dresser, which we bought at auction, is a late 18th-century Welsh oak piece, probably from Carmarthenshire. Our little 1850s cottage has a funny way of rejecting anything too grand or not right for the house. It prefers country furniture, and the house and the dresser seem to get along well.

Brown furniture is currently out of fashion and can be bought relatively cheaply, including early-colonial dressers. In the 1980s I can remember seeing prices as long as telephone numbers on dressers in smart High Street dealers. For years I looked for a dresser without seeing anything I liked, then about a decade ago, not one but two dressers came up in the weekly auction at Leonard Joel. They were both oak, both beautiful and both 18th century, and either of them would fit along the wall in our dining room. One was a bit more refined; the other, in unrestored condition, was kind of chunky with a great patina.

The chunky dresser was described as 'Oak Welsh dresser c. 1730'. It had four shelves for plates and three drawers at the front with original brass hardware. Below the drawers was a scalloped dress front, and there was an open shelf at the bottom – the perfect place to store baskets and bottles of wine. Although it was a little battered and missing a corner or two, and there was a crack in the oak plank on the top, it had bags of character. I prefer antiques that are not over-restored: for me, a bit of grime on them from years of use adds to their charm.

The only problem was that I was in the country looking at two images on a computer screen, and the dressers were on show in the city. I wasn't going to be able to get to a pre-auction viewing. After a bit of deliberation, I left an absentee bid on the chunky oak dresser – the other one was a bit too refined for our cottage.

When the auction house rang to tell me that my bid had been successful, I quickly called our local 'guy with a truck'. He picked up the dresser and left it covered with an old tarp in our garage. I got home late from my job that day and nervously lifted the tarp; the dresser was more beautiful than I could have imagined. A quick wipe-down with a clean cloth was all it needed before we moved it into our dining room. Words can't really describe the glow of the oak – over 200 years of waxing and polishing have given it a warm, mellow patina.

Many years of scouting flea markets and junk shops had left me with a large collection of old china and Staffordshire pottery, so the shelves were quickly filled. In many houses, miscellaneous

OPPOSITE
*Welsh oak dresser, c. 1730*

objects – letters, cards, photographs, spare dog collars, candles – seem to find their way to the dresser, and this is what happened to us. I love these accumulations of objects. A solar-powered plastic figure of the Queen that waves when sunlight hits it, Victorian copper jelly moulds, Staffordshire figures and dogs, ceramic ointment jars, blue-and-white china, silver, majolica plates, an early toby jug with a smirk on his face, a Russian blue-and-white frog brought back from a trip to Moscow and a Wedgwood cheese dome – all were added to our dresser to make it look 'right'.

Gifts have also taken up residence – we have two watercolours of our dogs, a pair of begonia-leaf plates from a fellow dresser owner, and from Mum's dresser we have a jug with a whippet handle. Seeds from the garden are hastily stored in bowls or old envelopes and pushed in among the china. As with most dressers, one drawer contains bits and pieces such as screwdrivers, tea strainers, sticky tape, candle stubs and spare light globes – all the stuff essential to modern life. The middle drawer holds dinner napkins and placemats and big serving spoons. The third drawer is a bit hard to open – a quirk of the dresser – so this is where we put things we don't use very often; it also contains a set of French transfer dinner plates. The potboard holds baskets of overflow china, vases and big salad bowls and platters – items that are easier to get to if they are on the dresser and not at the back of a cupboard. The drinks department has also set itself up at one end of the potboard, with bottles of gin and wine and Aperol.

None of the objects are particularly precious or rare, but it all adds to the charm of our dining room. Our dresser has become another member of the family, and I can't imagine living without it.

OPPOSITE
*Dressers look best crammed with china.*

# AN
# ELEGANT
# OAK
# DRESSER

---

## KAYE
## PICKETT

Antique dealer Kaye Pickett had been looking for a dresser for a long time before she bought this one. She'd been on a buying trip to the United Kingdom, and even though she saw hundreds of dressers, none were exactly what she wanted. She brought back a 40-foot container full of English furniture but no dresser. Then, on a chance trip to Graham Geddes Antiques in Melbourne, she found exactly what she had been looking for.

This very refined oak dresser was made around 1780, making it George III, and it has a gorgeous colour and patina. It is simple and elegant, and even though it's a big piece of furniture, it doesn't dominate the room or feel heavy. Kaye says there is a name, 'J Roberts', somewhere on the dresser.

The dresser has three drawers, each with two brass handles and cockbeading (a raised bead moulding that protects the edges on drawer fronts and creates shadow lines). The base features four elegant turned legs and three ogee arches with cockbeading. The potboard sits on little bracket feet that allow you to see under the dresser and help give it a feeling of lightness. The plate rack is simple, with wide backing boards.

Kaye's collection of 18th- and 19th-century pewter looks impressive against the dark oak boards, and two early Chinese export porcelain plates inject colour and interest into the composition. Like the dresser, Kaye's display is refined and perfectly at home in its graceful Georgian setting.

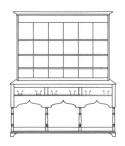

OPPOSITE
*Welsh oak dresser, c. 1780*

LEFT
*Detail showing ogee arches and cockbeading, the raised bead of timber around the drawers and arches.*

23

# BLUE-AND-WHITE ABUNDANCE

---

## JANET NIVEN

Nineteenth-century blue-and-white transfer ware fills this dresser to overflowing in the kitchen of Janet Niven's Sydney home. The dresser is pine, 19th century, and most likely English. It has unusual ventilation holes drilled in the cupboard doors, which slide rather than open on hinges, and three drawers across the front. The pediment moulding is only on the front – it doesn't continue around the sides – which indicates that the dresser would have originally been built into a kitchen or slotted between other pieces of furniture. It's a good height, so it can fit extra-large meat platters and hold a substantial amount of crockery.

For fifty years Janet has been a dealer of miniature portraits, blue-and-white transfer ware and 18th- and 19th-century ceramics and samplers. Most of the big English pottery manufacturers produced lines of blue and white, and different patterns were produced for different countries and markets, so there are many patterns to collect. Janet has a mixture of pieces on her dresser: Indian sporting scenes, Caramanian, Herculaneum, Liverpool and rarer patterns.

Cow creamers, most likely from Yorkshire, graze along the shelves of the plate rack, pierced blue-and-white chestnut baskets sit among early Staffordshire figures, and china animals break up the collection and add an element of whimsy. The odd ceramic ointment pot and lustreware mug have found a home on the dresser, and a collection of bone apple corers fills a copper lustre mug – not something you see every day. Either side of the dresser, draining plates from large meat platters hang on the wall to visually extend the blue-and-white theme through the room.

Nothing here is ugly or mundane: it all delights the eye. Janet is a master of display who understands symmetry, has the collector's instinct and knows the joy of living with her collection.

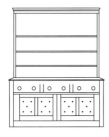

OPPOSITE
*Pine dresser, 19th century*

# THE ARTISTS' DRESSER

——

## CHELLY AND PETER GRAY

This rather monumental Australian-made Victorian-era painted dresser resides in the kitchen of Peter and Chelly Gray, artists who for the past twenty years have been producing metal and wire sculptures and objects. The couple are great collectors as well as makers of objects, and many of their finds come to the kitchen dresser and live there for a while.

The Grays bought the dresser from a dealer who acquired it from Wombat Park, a large old house in Daylesford, Victoria, when that house was renovated. It is painted in a 'kitchen cream' colour with a contrasting sludgy green on the knobs, the trim on the cupboard doors and the kickboard at the base. Lozenge shapes cut in the cupboard doors are backed with panels of zinc mesh to provide ventilation and, importantly in a country kitchen, to keep the cupboards vermin proof. The top of the base is quite high and the shelves on the plate rack are relatively wide, so there's plenty of room to display objects.

The dresser fits perfectly into the couple's 1860s cottage, which they have renovated. They have created a kitchen with antique fittings and recycled items, and the dresser looks as though it is original to the house.

In his spare time, Peter collects wirework. He has arguably the best collection in Australia – in fact, it has its own gallery building in the garden. Wirework baskets from the collection crown the dresser and run down one side.

Like a lot of dresser owners, the Grays change their display regularly. Chelly takes great care in curating her displays and there's always something to delight the eye: eggs, birds' nests, feathers, metal objects, small pieces of wirework, stacks of mixing bowls and breadboards. There might even be a display of vegetables made by the couple from patinated copper.

Here, Chelly has kept the colour palette pared back to whites, creams and neutral tones and the china and ceramics are mostly plain, which gives the display a relaxed and calm yet sophisticated feel. One of the couple's sculpted chooks, her plumage made from recycled bits and pieces of rusted and aged metal, sits quietly on a wire and metal nest.

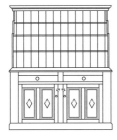

OPPOSITE
*Australian painted dresser, 18th century*

Chelly changes the display
on her dresser regularly,
and those with sharp eyes
might notice the different
arrangements on her dresser.

# COTTAGES
# AND
# CASTLES

---

# CHRISTINE
# REID

It's always fascinating seeing other people's collections, to see what they love and sense the passion behind their collection, to understand more about it and what makes the collector tick. Christine Reid, a garden writer, collects Staffordshire cottages and castles dating from 1820 to 1860, and displays these to great effect on a Welsh oak high dresser from Glamorganshire, c. 1760. It has an open plate rack, cup hooks, a five-drawer base and a central arch, with four turned supports above a potboard.

The whimsical little cottages and castles have abundant charm and make you stop and look. They were created as money boxes and pastille burners by many companies, including Spode, Worcester, Wedgwood, Derby and Davenport. In the Georgian and Regency periods, before modern sanitation and deodorants, burning pastilles was a way of masking nasty smells. Gentlefolk were embarrassed by noxious odours, and the fashion was for these miniature buildings that could fill your home with pleasant aromas. Smoke produced from the slowly smouldering pastilles would gently waft up the chimneys of the little homes, completing the effect of a miniature house.

Some of Christine's pieces commemorate famous cottages and houses; others show a cottage or house where an infamous gruesome murder of the time took place. Cheery stuff! Christine's favourite is a rare Chinese pagoda modelled on the Earl of Shrewsbury's pagoda in his garden at Staffordshire.

Green majolica plates form a dark backdrop for the cottages and castles, and Christine also displays Staffordshire figures and birds. Two Staffordshire horses with jockeys sit at the top of the dresser, looking as if they have raced each other there, and a large Sunderland masonic lustre jug sits on the potboard. Two fabulous Eric Ravilious coronation mugs on a lower shelf bring a more modern note to the arrangement along with a couple of Isis Ceramics blue-and-white plates – modern interpretations of 17th- and 18th-century Delftware plates. A vase of roses from the garden completes the display on this stylish and individual collector's dresser.

---

OPPOSITE
*Welsh oak high dresser, c. 1760*

# LARGE
# AND
# LOADED

—

Tucked away in a quiet corner of Hobart is the 1820 home of Anna and her husband. The heavily encrusted dresser of large proportions in the sitting room is the first thing you see when you walk in the front door. Pine and probably English c. 1820, it has three deep drawers with ebonised knobs. Small telltale signs indicate that it was probably painted at some stage in its life. There is no potboard – it's more of a table base – but that means there is space for some of Anna's pottery collection.

Anna has a passion for china, and you can certainly see that in the wonderful display on the dresser. The shelves groan with blue-and-white, green-and-white and other random pieces, displayed in her very individual way. Items are arranged in graduated stacks on the dresser top, and layers of plates lean against the backboard of the plate rack. The cup hooks are filled with cups, jugs and the odd tiny teapot. The whole effect is mesmerising, and when you walk past there is a gentle rattle of china and the cups and jugs sway lightly on their hooks. Anna's favourite piece is a small Delft tile from the 1600s featuring an elephant painted in a few clever, energetic brushstrokes. It sits in pride of place on the dresser.

Anna also has a smaller painted kitchen dresser put together by her husband. He added a plate rack to a chest of drawers to create a handy kitchen assistant that holds mugs, jugs and teapots, as well as oils, vinegars, salts and sauces, so they are at hand when someone is cooking.

OPPOSITE
*Pine dresser, c. 1820*

OPPOSITE
*Small painted dresser,
early 20th century*

40

# THE
# HOUSE
# WITH
# SEVEN
# DRESSERS

---

## VAL
## HAWKES

Val Hawkes collects a myriad of things, including blue-and-white china, pottery, stoneware, porcelain and children's items. She displays her collections on several dressers – seven so far – throughout her early-colonial house.

Val's kitchen has not one but two dressers, one of Olympic proportions, the other much smaller. The large dresser is Huon pine, its top a single slab 75 centimetres wide. It holds a prodigious amount of blue-and-white china, pottery and stoneware. Six comports run the length of the dresser top, filled with fruit and walnuts from the garden. The smaller dresser holds blue-and-white plates and rows and rows of the current year's preserves and jams.

One of the things Val collects is the mauve sprigged china known as Blue Betty, which she displays on a little modern painted dresser in a hallway. Upstairs is her collection of children's things – dolls, games, bears – featuring three children's dressers decked out in miniature china, including a miniature Blue Betty tea set.

Back downstairs in a sitting room is another dresser, a Welsh oak piece that probably dates from the 18th century, laden with Delft and early blue-and-white and Chinese export porcelain as well as some fascinating scrimshaw by Val's partner, Kim Akerman.

Val is a connoisseur with an eye for witty, vibrant displays. This vast array of goods, showcased in dressers from capacious to tiny, is proof of her passion.

OPPOSITE
*Large Huon pine dresser,
19th century*

OPPOSITE
*A plate rack is used to great effect to display some of Val's collectables.*

RIGHT
*Small Huon pine dresser, 19th century*

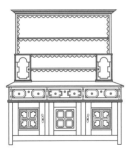

OPPOSITE
*Welsh oak dresser, 18th century*

FOLLOWING
*Particle-board dresser with collection of Blue Betty china, late 20th century*

49

OPPOSITE & RIGHT
*A trio of toy dressers, probably homemade as presents for children, c. early 20th century*

# DRESSERS MANY AND VARIED

## KELLY MOTT

The houses of collectors are always exciting to visit, and Kelly Mott's home in an old masonic hall is no exception. Kelly collects all sorts of things to do with kitchens and food preparation: butter churns, meat safes, scales, ice chests, china, silver, dressers. Her greatest passion is for enamel, and her collection includes jugs, teapots, coffee pots, mugs, buckets, and rows of kitchen canisters in both plain and graniteware enamel. The huge old hall gives Kelly plenty of display space, and her six dressers, a few meat safes and an old decorative ice chest are all pressed into service.

Kelly's dressers, which date from the 19th or early 20th century and are made from various timbers, show the huge variety of forms evident in Australia. On entering the house, the first dresser you see is a big one with twelve drawers. It may have started its life in a colonial shop and now happily stores a substantial chunk of Kelly's enamelware collection.

In the kitchen, a dresser with zinc mesh cupboard doors is a cross between a dresser and a food safe, surely an Australian variation, built to store dishes, china and food all in the one piece of furniture. In the laundry, a tall, painted Barossa dresser in a pleasing shade of distressed oxblood shows the German influence on dressers in Australia. Near the back door is a dresser that belonged to a Barossa Valley settler who went off to World War I and never returned. The original glass in the doors is gone, but the dresser still happily holds part of Kelly's collection. In another hallway near the back door is a piece cobbled together from an old chest of drawers and a glazed cupboard – not a dresser, but a make-do measure for storing and displaying blue-and-white china.

The big dresser, as Kelly calls it, is a Victorian or Edwardian piece from what must have been a very large house. It holds a huge amount of china; two rows of Asiatic pheasant platters, tureens and vegetable dishes; enamelware; and silverware. Over the years it has been painted and stripped, which only adds to its rustic charm.

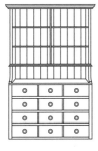

OPPOSITE & FOLLOWING (LEFT)
*Detail of a probable shop fitting piece, now used as a dresser, 19th century*

An old ice chest used for storage.

Kelly has cobbled together a glazed cupboard and an old rustic chest of drawers to create a makeshift dresser, 19th century.

57

Large Edwardian painted dresser,
late 19th or early 20th century

RIGHT
Barossa Valley painted dresser
with glazed doors (glass lost
long ago), early 20th century

59

*Barossa Valley dresser with original
paint, late 19th century*

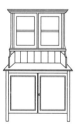

*Dresser with zinc-mesh
food-safe base, 19th century*

# THE GARDENER'S DRESSER

## MICHAEL DALE

Walking into Michael Dale's kitchen, you are immediately struck by the well-stocked elm-and-oak dresser that shares a nook with a big farmhouse table. It's a comfortable spot for afternoon tea or to sit and read.

The chunky elm top of the base has bowed over the years, giving the dresser great character. Dating from the late 18th or early 19th century, this English dresser was bought from a Melbourne dealer years ago. Over the years handles have been replaced, which is not unusual as tastes and fashions change.

The kitchen doesn't have much storage space, so the six-drawer, two-cupboard dresser holds all the cooking utensils, a box of cutlery, table linen and wineglasses. One cupboard contains a rather wonderful collection of jugs. It's a practical, hardworking piece of furniture as well as being decorative. Calico shopping bags hang in a relaxed manner from the plate rack, ready for a trip to the shops, and a lamp provides atmosphere and gives a warm glow in the evening.

Michael is a gardener, so there are always plants on the dresser – today it's a couple of begonias and a Chinese money plant. The top of the base looks like a well-tended garden bed with vegetables ready to harvest. There are two china tureens in vegetable form – a cabbage and a cauliflower – both presents from a dear friend; majolica leaf plates and majolica flower plates add to the garden theme. Birds sit on the plate rack above, and a pair of china hares hide in the greenery, waiting for the chance to nibble on the china vegetables when the kitchen is quiet.

On closer examination you can see a set of blue kingfisher plates from the much-missed Melbourne shop Izzi & Popo, and two Spode 'Christopher Wren' bird plates. After a while you notice a small taxidermy bird on the very top of the dresser, peeking out from a set of crystal lustre candlesticks. He looks rather like he has escaped from one of the plates and come to life.

OPPOSITE
*Elm-and-oak dresser,
c. 18th century*

# AT
# HOME
# IN
# THE
# KITCHEN

—

## MAY
## PETSCHEL

You could be forgiven for thinking you're in Europe rather than hot, dusty Australia when you walk into May Petschel's atmospheric kitchen. Copper pans hang on the walls and a dough-bin (kneading) table fills the centre of the room, with two narrow benches for sitting on. An old-fashioned light globe with a milk-glass shade hangs from the ceiling and the smell of freshly baked peanut butter and chocolate chip biscuits is in the air. This is definitely a non-built-in kitchen with great style, like the lady of the house.

May has not one but two dressers in the kitchen, both painted in the moody British Paints colour Black Ace. One was cleverly constructed by a local craftsman to incorporate an antique enamel kitchen sink with brass taps that were original to the kitchen. The other, a marriage of an old sideboard, a glazed bookcase cupboard and two sets of antique sewing machine drawers, is on the opposite wall. The different components work well, and you could be forgiven for thinking it is a European kitchen dresser. In fact, it's a creation by May, painted to match the other dresser.

May collects old pewter and tinware, which she sets off with select pieces of white and cream stoneware and china. Special pieces fill the shelves of her sink dresser, and the arrangements of quiet, considered dark objects against the dark background bring to mind Flemish still-life paintings. May is a dedicated antique hunter and has bought kitchenalia from Ryn England (see page 99) and a wonderful copper cabbage from Chelly and Peter Gray (see page 29).

The other dresser holds the china and glassware of daily life, with little drawers storing all manner of kitchen supplies and spices. A huge mortar and pestle, surely from an old pharmacy, sits on the open middle shelf and contains fresh fruit.

This is the kitchen of a cook, and everything in the room, including both dressers, is used all day, every day. As May works, bakes and washes dishes at her sink dresser, in a beautiful charcoal-grey linen apron, she becomes part of the still life.

OPPOSITE
*Edwardian painted dresser with enamel sink set into its top, early 20th century*

69

PREVIOUS
*May has combined a sideboard, glazed cabinet and two sets of sewing machine drawers to create a custom-made dresser.*

OPPOSITE
*Barossa Valley pine dresser, 19th century*

RIGHT
*Dresser with glazed doors, early 20th century*

# A
# FINE
# WELSH
# OAK
# DRESSER

## NEIL
## ROBERTSON

This particularly fine dresser, c. 1750 and attributed to the Vale of Glamorgan in southern Wales, belonged to the late Neil Robertson, a renowned collector of antiques, art and curios. It shows just how attractive a Welsh oak dresser can be, with its silhouette supports, beautifully shaped apron, and fine colour and patina. It sits lightly in the room and doesn't feel like a bulky piece of furniture – rather, it feels sleek and refined.

The open-back potboard dresser with its slightly bowed shelves shows off its collections to fine effect. All of Neil's favourite pieces are to be found there: a truly stunning and balanced collection of blue-and-white transfer plates, Staffordshire figures and animals, two silver Mauchline ware moneyboxes in the form of small cottages, green glass paperweights (also known as dumps) and a whimsical model of a loaf of bread with the words 'O Lord' painted on it. A model butter churn – a salesperson's sample – sits on the bottom shelf.

Neil's home was filled with rare and wonderful things. Tabletops were covered with arrangements of 18th-century snuffboxes, while walls were lined with paintings and literally hundreds of silhouettes and portrait miniatures. The dresser sat next to a big gate-leg table with a set of comfortable Windsor chairs. Staffordshire cats and figures were perched on the shelves while a pair of superior black cats peered down from atop the dresser to watch their master as he sat at the table and did the crossword. The dresser and its treasures celebrate Neil's lifelong love of antiques and his discerning collector's eye.

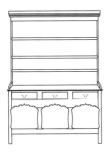

OPPOSITE
*Welsh oak dresser, c. 1750*

# BEGONIAS
# AND
# A
# GNOME

---

## NGAIRE
## AND
## ROGER
## HUDSON

A fine and rare Bosley Pottery gnome stands guard over the many and varied collections in the dining room of Ngaire and Roger Hudson's home. He watches over their early miner's cottage in central Victoria from his vantage point on the Australian colonial shield-doored dresser – a clever find by the pair years ago at an antique fair in Bendigo. Its diminutive size means it fits perfectly into a niche beside the fireplace and looks like it was built for the spot.

Australian pottery dominates this room of the house. The collection is beautifully displayed on the dresser, on a plate rack, on a meat safe and on the mantelpiece. Bigger pieces rest on the floor. Pottery koalas at the top of the small dresser preside over gumleaf vases and an extraordinary glazed Australian 'Abbott' water filter.

Off the dining room is a room dedicated to the couple's majolica collection, where two dressers face each other and show some, but by no means all, of the pieces. The dressers are similar to the one in the dining room – Australian, but larger – and hold all manner of majolica items, from cheese domes to sardine dishes. There is a row of Chinese temple birds, all glazed in dark green but each different and full of personality. The two shelves below contain plates, dishes and cake stands, all paying homage to the Victorian obsession with botany, especially begonias. The begonia plates and dishes show huge variations of colours and leaf forms and, like lots of collections, look great displayed en masse.

The dresser opposite holds an array of plates, bowls, dishes, bird jugs and fish 'glug' jugs (they make a wonderful 'glug' sound as you pour liquid from them). An ancient glass-cased taxidermy kookaburra and an equally ancient taxidermy sulphur-crested cockatoo, both purchased years ago from a local antique bush fair, have taken up residence on top. On the table in the middle of the room are new pieces and items that haven't yet found a place.

The displays on the three dressers in the house changes as Ngaire and Roger's collection grows and takes different directions.

OPPOSITE
*Australian pine colonial dresser with shield-shaped doors, 19th century*

81

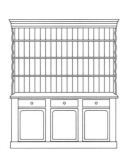

DOGS
MUST NOT BE BROU[...]
INTO THE ROOM

# ECHOES OF COLONIAL AUSTRALIA

---

## NATASHA ALVEY

Natasha Alvey lives in country Victoria in a home filled with antiques. She has a great eye, grouping and displaying her collection in a modern and graphic way – she understands scale.

In the kitchen is a dark-glazed, almost black 19th-century dresser. It houses some of Natasha's blue-and-white china and a fascinating collection of old pharmacy and apothecary jars, bottles and pots with worn and aged labels, and a rack of old test tubes. The display sits safely inside the glazed doors of the dresser, looking for all intents and purposes like the tools of the trade of an alchemist.

Around the corner in the dining area is an Australian early-colonial painted pine dresser. It has solid shield-shaped doors on the top, diagonally planked doors on the bottom, and two drawers in the middle. In early-colonial Australia, solid doors on your dresser kept the dust and vermin of the outback away from your china (dust storms in Natasha's part of the country are not uncommon). The diagonal boards give the dresser a nice graphic twist and loads of personality, and the soft green and yellow paint finish reflects the colours of the Australian bush. The unpainted shelves hold Fowlers Vacola preserving jars, stoneware, china and jelly moulds. The dresser has a few mends: bits of tin have been nailed to the top, reflecting the bush ethos of repair, mend and make do.

OPPOSITE
*Detail of dresser with glazed doors, early 20th century*

Painted farm dresser with
homespun metal repairs,
19th century

# LAYERS
# OF
# TREASURES

——

## TARA
## BADCOCK

Artist Tara Badcock lives with her husband and two children in the picturesque small town of Chudleigh in northern Tasmania. Her painted dresser was bought in Launceston, and Tara believes it dates from around 1910 and was made in Tasmania. The base has zinc mesh on the sides for ventilation and to keep pests and vermin out, so at one time it must have been used as a pantry cupboard.

Tara has layered the dresser with finds from markets, vintage stores and antique shops. The whole effect is one of joyful abundance. She has maximised the storage space on the shelves by overlapping plates – a real stroke of genius that means she is able to show lots of her collection at once. Stacks of teacups on the first shelf down from the top add to the art of the display. Tara's favourite pieces include a teapot painted with stylised flowers on the middle shelf; some Chinese export porcelain cups; finds from a Paris street market; and a red and grey Russian teacup, given to her by a friend, hanging from one of the cup hooks. The top of the dresser has a display of silver-plated teapots and a coffee pot, nicely capped off by an old galvanised-iron vent from a vent pipe.

On opening the cupboard doors you can see more of Tara's collection of ceramics, with piles of dinner plates, bowls, tureens and jelly moulds awaiting their turn on the dresser. On the wall next to the dresser, a 'Felix the Cat' clock, which belongs to Tara's son Felix, adds more personality and an element of humour to the display.

OPPOSITE
*Tasmanian dresser, c. 1910*

# A PAINTED DRESSER

—

# RYN ENGLAND

This charming green Depression-era dresser lives in Ryn England's cottage in Maryborough, Victoria. The blue-green Australian-made dresser came from a dealer in Inglewood, 40 kilometres north-west of Bendigo, and is constructed in one piece, like an Irish dresser. Its only ornamentation is bevelled edges on the thick timber panels on the cupboard doors and two white ceramic knobs on the drawers. It's not a huge dresser, so it probably came from a worker's cottage. It fits perfectly into Ryn's cottage kitchen.

Ryn, who is a dealer in antiques and vintage items and specialises in kitchenalia, loves the colour of the dresser, the cracked patina of its old thick paint, and the way the topcoat is slowly wearing off to reveal a blue layer underneath. Painted furniture has a charm of its own, and Ryn has a collection of pared-back painted pieces in her cottage. She is extremely disciplined about not keeping many of her finds – they go to her stall at Mill Markets in Daylesford, where she trades under the name Whisk and Wheelbarrow.

Ryn's dresser displays her collection of white china and ceramics. She brings a contemporary look to it by including some modern pieces by her mother, Glenn England, a potter. The sculptural quality of the items on the dresser can be appreciated due to the restricted colour palette, and the contrast of the shades of white against the blue-green is very pleasing. All the china in Ryn's kitchen is put to use – nothing is just for display – and the dresser drawers are full of kitchen implements.

A few special pieces stand out: a clotted cream jar printed in a classic typeface and a Bynol jar with its original type. (Bynol was a mixture of malt and cod-liver oil that was taken as a nutritional supplement. It sounds rather unappetising by today's standards!) A 'Save milk' ceramic disc – an ingenious device that, when placed in the bottom of a saucepan, stops heated milk from boiling over – sits on the top shelf, and two old silver teapots finish off the pared-back country aesthetic nicely.

Ryn shares the cottage with her dogs, Banjo the whippet and Hazel the rescue dog. Banjo is perfectly colour-matched to the china on the dresser.

OPPOSITE
*Australian-made dresser with original paint, early 20th century*

HARRIS'
ORIGINAL PURE
CLOTTED CREAM
FROM
DEVONSHIRE
DAILY

# TWO COUNTRY HOUSE DRESSERS

## MICHAEL McWILLIAM AND ROBERT HENLEY

Old country houses and dressers seem to go hand in hand, and lots of larger country houses have more than one of these enduring and much-loved pieces of furniture. Michael McWilliam and Robert Henley's Georgian country house is no exception. It is filled with lovely things and has atmosphere with a capital A. The house is in original condition and Michael and Robert have a light touch, so there have been no aggressive renovations.

Under the staircase on the way to the kitchen is a simple dresser full of Australian early-colonial pottery. Vases, jugs, cachepots and an army of pottery frogs line the shelves and a plate rack sits on a simple table base with one drawer. The subtle mottled glazes of the pottery suit the warm timber of the dresser.

Walk through a glass door into the kitchen and there, fitting neatly into an alcove beside the fireplace, is another dresser. It's a glowing 18th-century English oak example, featuring six drawers with cockbeading, two cupboards, and bone key escutcheons. A row of treacle-glaze (sometimes also known as Rockingham glaze) jugs and salt-glaze pottery pieces fill the top of the dresser, and green majolica plates and objects line two shelves of the plate rack. One of the three pressed-glass elephant salt dishes belonged to Michael's mother, and Robert found the other two many years later; the trio now live very happily together on the middle shelf. A row of Australian pottery vases and horticultural award plates is on the top shelf.

To the back of the kitchen is a walk-in pantry filled with more of Michael and Robert's collection, which they rotate on display around the house. An oak kitchen table is set in front of the oak dresser, and you can sit here with a cup of tea and admire the show.

OPPOSITE
*English oak dresser, 18th century*

Table and plate-rack dresser,
19th century

# THE DRESSER AT FOSS

—

## MICHELLE HYLAN AND CLIFF PANNAM

A small note reading 'No BoDee Loves Mee' takes centre stage on Michelle Hylan and Cliff Pannam's dresser in their country home, Foss. Written by their son William when he was quite young, it is tucked into a silver-framed photograph of him as a baby.

The French provincial dresser from Montpellier, c. 1840s, is made from chestnut wood and stands at 2.26 metres high. It has solid brass fittings and large cupboards with drawers above that give plenty of storage space. The couple bought it about twenty years ago from an antique shop in Geelong, and since then it's lived in a couple of houses with them. It's definitely part of the family.

Cookbooks dominate this dresser in a house full of good food, books and conversation. Michelle keeps her favourite cookbooks on it so they are close at hand when needed, and pots and pans fill the generous cupboards.

The dresser is probably the most used piece of furniture in the house. It works as Michelle's office in the kitchen – she keeps her diary and car keys on it, and treasured family photos end up here along with all sorts of other things. A stack of baskets lives on top; straw hats for gardening sit on the upper shelf, ready to be grabbed on the way out the door; and a number-one rosette by textile artist Tara Badcock (see page 95) is pinned to the top right-hand corner, as if it's been awarded to the best and most loved dresser. The lower shelf holds more cookbooks and a row of photos in silver frames.

The right-hand drawer contains Michelle's secret stash of tools, as she is the person who repairs things in the household: there are screws and screwdrivers, pliers, a hammer, nails, duct tape and other fix-it stuff. Michelle is also a great gardener – she produces armloads of peonies in spring – so there is usually a vase of homegrown flowers on the dresser.

Bundles of champagne cages sit on the top shelf, a testament to the enjoyment of life at Foss. They are waiting to be turned into little chairs by Michelle to give to friends and visitors. Many will end up on dressers around the country and overseas as mementos of a visit to Foss.

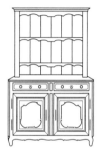

OPPOSITE
*French provincial dresser, c. 1840*

Mementos of family life
fill the dresser.

# SCRIMSHAW AND WHALEBONE

---

# PETER WOOF

Colonial antique dealer and collector Peter Woof lives and works in Evandale in north-eastern Tasmania. His shop is a stopping-off point for many collectors, as it is always stocked with superb furniture and choice objects.

Peter's home is furnished with a beautifully restrained selection of colonial furniture. His cedar dresser is of very small proportions and must have been made for a tiny cottage. It dates from around 1830 and is in unrestored condition. Unrestored pieces from such an early date are rare – Peter saved this one from a backyard dealer who was just about to take to it with a belt sander to refinish it.

The little dresser wears its knocks and bumps with pride. Somewhere along the way an inventive person has added a wooden peg with a button on the top to 'peg' the doors closed. Turned feet raise the dresser off the ground and give it a light appearance.

Peter's passion is scrimshaw, especially Australian colonial-era carved whale teeth and whalebone. His pieces sit well on the little cedar dresser, as if it had been made for this purpose. A carved pan bone (the lower jawbone of a whale) on the bottom shelf shows two sailing ships at sea, while the middle shelf holds a row of carved whale teeth featuring delicate views of ships and boats and seabirds, and portraits of wives and sweethearts.

On the top shelf you can see small bone baskets that were used as pincushions, and some carved corset stays known as busks. Busks were decorated by scrimshaw artists and often given to their wives or sweethearts as love tokens.

OPPOSITE
*Early-colonial cedar dresser, c. 1830*

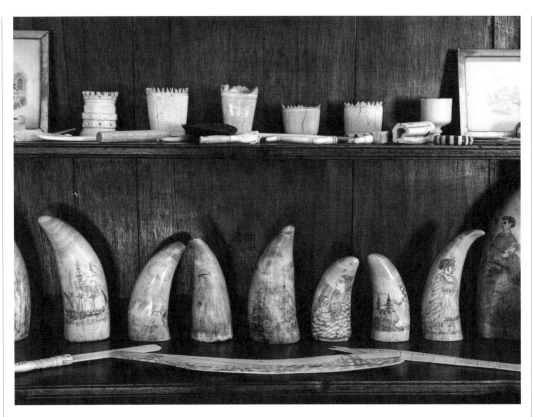

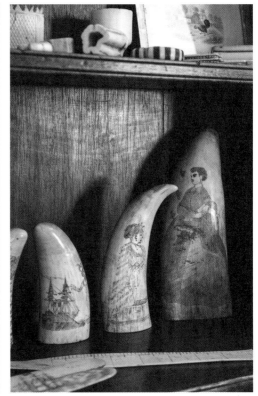

h=H
enrhumé
yacinthe
gaieté
damner
emment
emment
orgueil
72 BIS

# MEMORIES AND STORIES

## GLENNY EASTWOOD

A vintage wind-up toy tin 'chook' and its chick keep watch over the treasures on Glenny Eastwood's dresser – an enviable collection of blue-and-white china, china doll parts, ceramic jelly moulds, enamel boxes and antique children's toys. Glenny's collection of interesting objects and small treasures is very personal and beautifully curated and displayed. Every shelf has something to delight the eye.

Glenny found her dresser ten years ago when, after a boozy lunch, she ventured into an antique shop in Trentham, Victoria. She left a deposit on the dresser straight away – it was exactly what she had been looking for. Way too big for the small miner's cottage that she and her partner, Daniel, lived in, it had to be put into storage for a few years while they figured out what to do. Daniel ended up building a room onto the cottage to house it.

Glenny is a keen traveller and whenever she goes on holiday, she is on the hunt for treasures to put on her dresser. Small items are easy to pack and bring home from trips, so many of her pieces come from British junk shops and markets. Each has a story attached to it of a day spent at a flea market, searching charity shops or at the (alas, now gone) Fryerstown Antique Fair in central Victoria, where 300 dealers would set up stalls under the gum trees and you could spend a whole weekend looking for treasures.

The pine dresser, which probably dates from the 19th century, has three deep drawers across the front and an unusual, almost-secret narrow drawer at each end. The plate rack has backing boards and the potboard is the perfect size to house Glenny's wealth of blue-and-white meat dishes. The shelves hold a large part of her blue-and-white china collection, including a good deal of Asiatic pheasant and willow pattern. There's also a quirky assortment of ceramic ointment, bloater-paste and marmalade pots from the days before plastic, when attractive ceramic jars and containers were used for food items and medicines. A cast-metal kangaroo sits amid a collection of other cast-metal animals on a dresser that holds a lot of memories and stories.

# A BATTLE-SCARRED DRESSER

## BIANKAH MILLER

Biankah Miller runs a homewares store in Red Cliffs, north-western Victoria, called The Collektive, where she carefully curates and sells an inspiring mix of new, antique and vintage pieces.

Her stout German-influenced dresser is a Barossa Valley piece that she brought home from the shop. When she bought it, it had been in someone's garage workshop for many years and was covered in a thick layer of old engine oil with stickers and transfers all over the glass doors. Biankah gave it a good scrub, gently scraped the oil company stickers off the doors, and removed the many years of accumulated dirt and motor oil to reveal the original cream and green paintwork with a splash of red paint, which Biankah says is her favourite part of the dresser. The deeply patinated paint only adds to its rustic charm.

Recovered from its exile, the dresser now takes pride of place in the Miller household. It stands on one side of the kitchen and holds Biankah's tea paraphernalia: collections of black-and-white transfer ware, Viceroy Tea branded cups and saucers, silver teapots and a great selection of teas. One of the small drawers below the doors is missing but that doesn't worry Biankah. She loves that the dresser wears its battle scars proudly and is living again as it was designed to – that is, as an important part of the family.

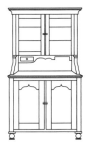

OPPOSITE
*Barossa Valley dresser with glazed doors, 19th century*

*Heavily patinated and distressed, the dresser wears its battle scars well.*

# OLD
# MEETS
# NEW

---

## DEBBIE
## AND
## CAMERON
## WILSON

A large stuffed goose stands in Debbie and Cameron Wilson's kitchen, catching you off guard when you walk in the door. Old meets new here: a gleaming stainless steel cooker and rangehood and a battery of French copper pots rub shoulders with the couple's 18th-century Welsh oak dresser.

The dresser sits on a floor of old flagstones laid by Cameron, who can build, repair or make anything. The floor seems like it has always been there, but then so does the dresser. Add to the equation Debbie's flair for putting a house together and you have an incredibly beautiful and individual home. Everything looks right.

The dresser, of particularly fine colour and very simple design, holds crockery and big glass jars of kitchen staples (flour, breadcrumbs, dried pasta), a plaited rope of garlic, copper kitchen moulds and early pewter pieces. Two long drawers with cockbeading sit over a potboard, making up the base. The only ornamentation is the central support, which has been cut into a vase or baluster shape in a small creative flourish that gives the piece great charm.

The plate rack has three shelves, and a row of blacksmith-made hooks runs along the top and makes a handy place to store decorative cooking implements. Three carved and painted wooden pigeons on top of the dresser look like they have just flown in the kitchen window for a quick visit or to peck at the jar of breadcrumbs.

OPPOSITE
*Welsh oak dresser, 18th century*

# SHOW-STOPPERS
———
## CORNELIUS HORGAN

This show-stopping 18th-century French pine dresser lives in designer Cornelius Horgan's dining room. Decorating the cupboard doors are medallions carved with classical profiles of a woman with a headdress of wheat and poppies, and a man with a headdress of grapes and vine leaves. Cornelius believes the dresser was once one of a pair, perhaps made for a restaurant, and that the medallions represent the seasons.

The medallion at the top of the dresser features another female profile – a portrait of the original owner of the piece, perhaps – and scrollwork on either side. Three shelves are held in place by chunky side supports and two drawers sit above the cupboards. Over time some of the pine has cracked, moved and split but this just adds to the dresser's charm.

This is a low-backed dresser, but it still manages to show a generous collection of Imari-style china that once belonged to Cornelius's business partner, Leslie Walford. A tureen and a set of four silver candlesticks complete the display. Cornelius says he uses the china all the time and it's nice to remember eating off it in Leslie's home.

The dresser is against a wall covered in Japanese woven bamboo paper, which has a subtle texture and shows off the piece handsomely. It sits on a custom green cork floor that plays off the green jug at the top of the dresser – a masterly touch. The cork tiles are warm in winter and give the room a freshness.

An imposing 18th-century French oak dresser is against another wall in the dining room. Cupboards on either side of a central plate rack feature carved floral sprays; the back of the plate rack is lined in a checked fabric and displays white china. This dresser has plenty of storage space, with two more huge cupboards and three drawers in the base.

Cornelius believes that decorative pieces such as dressers give presence to a room. Both of his dressers were bought from the legendary designer Ros Palmer, and they certainly make his dining room a special place.

OPPOSITE
*French pine dresser, 18th century*

OPPOSITE
*French oak dresser, 18th century*

135

# IMARI
# AND
# WEDGWOOD
—
# ALISON
# HAWKES

A veritable Imari army fills Alison Hawkes's Tasmanian-made Huon pine dresser – a typical one-drawer, one-spacious-cupboard dresser dating from the late 19th or early 20th century. The shelves sing with colour and pattern, and the porcelain's heavy gilding glints in the bright daylight of the sitting room. As you walk past, cups swing gently on the hooks, proudly showing off their patterns, rich colour and decorated interiors.

Many English ceramic houses manufactured wares inspired by Japanese Imari porcelains. Alison's collection is from the Derby palette, which was an English response produced for the English market. Alison says you get a lot of bang for your buck with Imari, and the richness of colour, pattern and gilding certainly looks impressive in such a large display. Most of Alison's pieces are red and blue with lashings of rich gilding, but she particularly loves the ones with green – and they do leap out at you. A row of differently patterned and gilded creamers sits on the top shelf.

Tucked away in the dining room is another very similar dresser containing a collection of Wedgwood's reasonably rare 'Fallow Deer' pattern in beautiful blue and white. Alison has been collecting this pattern piece by piece for many years. Layers of plates rest in the plate rack, and platters, vegetable dishes and bowls fill the rest of the dresser in a generous display.

OPPOSITE
*Imari porcelain fills this Tasmanian Huon pine dresser in a symphony of colour, pattern and heavy gilding.*

This Tasmanian Huon pine dresser is filled to overflowing with 'Fallow Deer' pattern, Wedgwood.

# THE FURNITURE MAKER'S DRESSERS

## ALLAN DAVIS

Furniture maker Allan Davis's kitchen in Hobart contains two dressers. One has a large base and is covered in its original crusty paint. Its plate rack has disappeared at some point. It came from a clearing sale at Stone House, a property near Oatlands in central-east Tasmania; it would have been built for the house in or around 1825 and lived there all its long life.

Allan's other kitchen dresser is a smaller Huon pine piece he discovered in an old workshop. It has a typical Tasmanian frieze at the top, one drawer, and two cupboards with turned wooden knobs and raised panels on the doors. An oil tin had been leaking into it for decades and the dresser was filthy when Allan found it. He says it oozes the odd bit of oil to this day. The dresser is home to the essentials of modern life: keys, mail, much-used cookbooks, a collection of electrical isolators, invitations to gallery openings, and a few of Allan's many decoy ducks, which he both makes and collects. The ducks seem to feature on every surface in his home.

A Cessna propeller leans nonchalantly against the smaller dresser – at first sight it could easily be mistaken for a sculpture. Maybe the rest of the plane is lurking in the huge workshop connected to Allan's home.

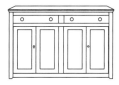

OPPOSITE
*Early-colonial painted and distressed dresser, c. 1825*

Huon pine dresser,
late 19th century

# FINDING
THE
ONE

---

## FLORIDA
AND
MILES
RICKARD-KERR

Florida Rickard-Kerr found her beautiful oak dresser, c. 1760–70, on an antique-buying trip to the United Kingdom with Kaye Pickett (see page 21). She saw it across a crowded warehouse full of antiques in Oxford and knew instantly it was the one.

The commanding dresser has six spice drawers along the bottom of the plate rack, six drawers in the base and two generous cupboards, all sitting on bracket feet. There are lozenge-shaped timber inlays between the drawers at the top of the base, and brass handles and inlaid diamond-shaped bone key escutcheons. The plate rack has unusually wide backing boards.

Florida and Miles's dresser takes pride of place in the sitting room of their home, displaying a large collection of classic blue-and-white willow pattern and Delft pieces. Florida was born in Delft and has a real love of their ceramics.

OPPOSITE
*Oak dresser, c. 1760–70*

# WESTBURY ANTIQUES

---

## HARVEY AND CAROL WILKINS

Harvey and Carol Wilkins live above their shop, Westbury Antiques, in Avoca, Victoria. Formerly a large bank, the shop stocks 17th-, 18th- and early 19th-century furniture and objects. The couple go on regular buying trips to Britain to find the treasures they sell, and have a dedicated group of loyal customers. A changing array of overflow pieces find places in their home every day. Harvey says it's great to live with a piece for a while and enjoy it, but it's also very satisfying to see it go to a new home where it will be loved.

Carol arranges the pieces in the shop so that each time you visit the display is different. There might be a group of particularly fine 18th-century toby jugs or some early pewter chargers (plates) or, even better, a collection of Measham 'Bargeware' teapots with rich treacle-like glaze, applied floral decoration and characteristic mini teapot finials. And there are usually one or two impressive oak dressers for sale.

Harvey has an encyclopaedic knowledge of antique furniture and can point out all sorts of fascinating details on the items they sell. He can explain the construction techniques and regional variations of different dressers and how the different timbers have been used.

One of Carol and Harvey's pieces is a beautiful Welsh deuddarn – a two-level storage cupboard – inlaid with its date of creation and a sun motif. It was once sold by the famous Mary Bellis, an antique dealer from Hungerford in England who specialised in early furniture and works of art, so it has impeccable provenance. Harvey says that a deuddarn and a dresser, along with a table and chairs, would have sufficed to furnish a cottage kitchen.

OPPOSITE
*Oak George III high dresser with mahogany cross-banded drawers, from Lancashire, c. 1760*

ABOVE & OPPOSITE
*Welsh cwpwrdd deuddarn
from Snowdonia, 1769*

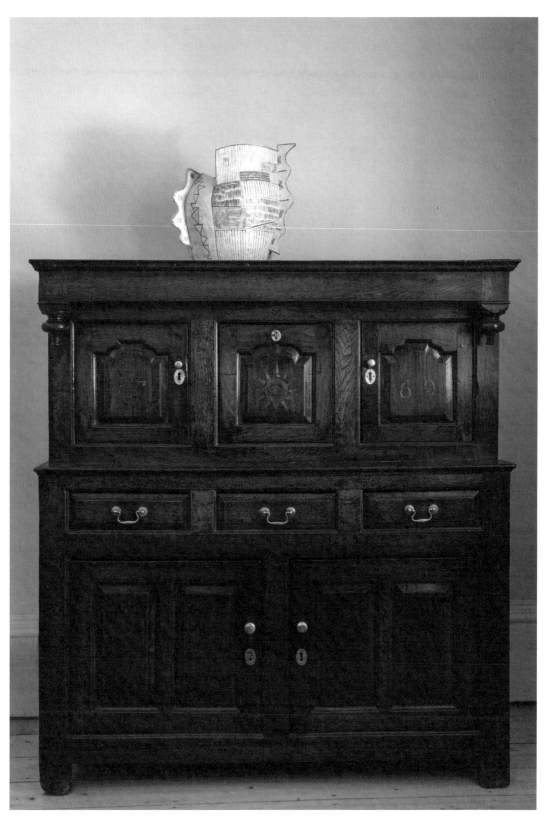

Welsh oak dresser with
spice drawers from
Carmarthenshire, c. 1760

OPPOSITE
*French painted dresser with
glazed doors, 19th century*

156

# MINIATURE DRESSERS

Miniature furniture and goods have a long history, and over the centuries miniature furniture has been made for various reasons. The pieces might be toys for children to teach them about running a home — these are usually simpler versions of the full-sized objects. Or they might be salespeople's samples for prospective furniture buyers to see a scale model before ordering a full-sized piece to be made by a cabinet-maker. Some of the highest-end furniture makers, such as Gillows in England, produced beautifully crafted miniature furniture as samples of what the company's craftsmen could produce. Apprentice pieces were also made, as a way for an apprentice cabinet-maker to show his woodworking skills and capabilities to a prospective employer.

Sometimes small pieces of furniture were made as a special order for an adult's doll's house. These items could cost as much as, or even more than, the same piece in full size. In 17th-century Netherlands, one way to show your wealth and status was to collect miniatures and display them in elaborate doll's houses.

Queen Mary's Dolls' House, designed by Sir Edwin Lutyens, the famous architect of the time, is an example of a high-end doll's house. Made between 1921 and 1924, it is filled with furniture and goods of the highest quality, commissioned from companies and makers of the day. The furniture was created from precious timbers and features minute detail. The kitchen contains two potboard dressers displaying a huge array of copper pots and pans, jelly moulds, mixing bowls, and a copper kettle made out of a George V penny.

Today the interest in miniatures has only increased, and there are makers worldwide and fairs and magazines devoted to the subject. It seems that people of all ages have a fascination with the world in miniature form.

This miniature Welsh oak potboard dresser with dovetailed drawers, backed with miniature boards, was either an apprentice piece or a salesperson's sample. It has been meticulously made to reflect all the construction details of a full-sized dresser, and perfectly suits this collection of miniature china.

# A CHILD'S DRESSER

## SHARON RANDALL

Toy dressers were popular items for children to play with in the 19th and early 20th centuries. What better way for a young girl to be introduced to having her own kitchen? Children's tea sets could be stored on a scaled-down children's dresser.

This child's dresser is part of Sharon Randall's collection and came from the estate of the late Mirka Mora, the much-loved Melbourne artist and doll collector, painter and maker. Sharon had met Mirka a number of times and remembers her as being rather exotic and lots of fun. Mirka lived surrounded by an extensive collection of handmade dolls and all the things that go with them – beds, prams, clothing, dolls' houses and a couple of children's dressers. Sharon bought this particular piece from the auction held after Mirka's death. It's probably a Depression-era piece made with love by someone for their daughter or granddaughter to play with. Timber has been reused from other items: you can still see the original labels from the Reckitt's Blue boxes that were recycled to make the drawers. (Reckitt's Blue was used when you were washing whites, to dye the rinse water and make the whites appear whiter. These days, modern detergents contain optical whiteners that do the same job, but Reckitt's Blue is still made.)

The dresser has three bottom cupboards, four drawers, and a plate rack with glass doors and a small lock and key. It is decorated with a pediment and lozenge shapes set on the cupboards. The whole thing is painted a 'kitchen cream' colour and the old paint is beginning to blister, which adds to the charm and patina of the piece. Sharon found the miniature china at Red Cart Vintage (see page 193). It is probably salesperson's samples rather than from a child's tea set, but it fits perfectly into the dresser.

OPPOSITE
*Toy dresser homemade from found timber, early 1930s*

# A
# FRENCH
# DRESSER

---

## NEXUS
## DESIGNS

This blue-painted dresser lives in a country home designed by Nexus Designs for a busy couple as an escape from city life and a place to unwind. The dresser is French, early 19th century, and was purchased by the owners from Graham Cornell Antiques. Graham painted the dresser a powdery blue that over the years has rubbed off to create a wonderful look. It houses a substantial collection of Limoges 'Monet' Giverny china by Robert Haviland & C. Parlon, based on an original design by Claude Monet in 1898 for use in his own home in Giverny. The collection was left to the couple by a close friend.

The dresser is near the dining table and also contains a few blue-and-white platters and a couple of pieces by local artist Bern Emmerichs. A jug by ceramicist Deborah Halpern sits in the middle of the upper shelf. Two Philippe Starck Miss Sissi lamps add to the mix of traditional meets modern and create mood in the evening. Nearby on the wall, a still-life painting by Sarah Faulkner cleverly echoes the colours of the dresser and its objects.

A bunch of roses from the garden and the bright, cheerful ceramics combine to give this dresser a contemporary, light feel that cleverly continues throughout the house.

# EVANDALE VILLAGE STORE

---

## CAROLYN IMLACH

The Evandale Village Store, near Launceston in Tasmania, has been operating more or less continuously since it was built in 1843. It still has its original timber counters, deep drawers and shelves, and owner Carolyn Imlach has added antique dressers to help display the merchandise.

Dressers work well for a store like this and fit the aesthetic perfectly. At any time there will be three or four dressers in the store, set up by Carolyn to display groups of items so that they tell a story. Today a large 19th-century dresser sits inside the door, stacked with jars of local honey, candles, ceramic jugs and other wares. Drawers are left half open to show lovely textured linens.

The stock comprises huge amounts of handmade artisanal goods from local, national and international producers, similar to how a colonial store would have operated. Shoppers need to do several laps to see and take in everything. The abundance of goods makes the Evandale Village Store feel like an alluring cave of treasures.

OPPOSITE
*Tasmanian pine dresser, 19th century*

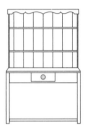

RIGHT
*Tasmanian Huon pine dresser,*
*19th century*

# THE DRESSER AT MULGOA COTTAGE

—

## JAMES BROADBENT

Mulgoa Cottage, built between 1810 and 1811, is the oldest inhabited house in Australia. It is the home of James Broadbent, and his dresser lives in the kitchen, which is built away from the main house – in early-colonial Australia, kitchens were built separate from houses to avoid the risk of fire.

This particular kitchen, built in 1907, is at least the third the house has had over the years. James recently rebuilt it and revived the dresser his father made for his mother in 1941, soon after they got married. After a while they bought another dresser and this one was retired to a shed in the garden. The base then spent thirty years on the verandah of James's cottage before finding its new home in his kitchen. The wooden top was rotting, so James replaced it with a slate hearthstone that fitted almost perfectly. The idea was to use as much of the original dresser as possible.

James isn't keen on fitted kitchens, so an old enamel sink was re-enamelled, and a smart draining rack over the sink holds pewter plates. The dresser houses all the china he uses in the kitchen as well as drinking glasses. All the cutlery, with handles made from deer antlers, is in two cutlery trays on the slate-topped base. The handles on the cupboards are cotton reels cut in half – a traditional 'make do' way of making handles. The shelves contain part of James's salt-glaze ceramic collection, pewter and a fine cow-jug creamer; the salt-glaze jars were once tobacco jars and now act as kitchen canisters.

James bought a wood-graining roller at a paint shop and did the graining on the cupboard doors himself. He wanted them to look decorative rather than like wood, and the subtle graining effect can be seen down the sides and in the middle of the upper cupboard. The colour was matched to wallpaper elsewhere in the house: James calls it 'Drab Green'. He likes dark spaces, so the walls in his very 'masculine' kitchen are painted charcoal grey. At first he thought it was too dark, but now he likes the way it brings out the green of the dresser.

OPPOSITE
*Australian dresser, homemade from reclaimed timber, 20th century*

# THE
# DRESSER
# IN
# THE
# SHED

---

# KIM
# ROWLATT

This fine Australian cedar dresser lives in a converted farm building in central Victoria and has been pressed into service in Kim Rowlatt's Queen Bee soap-making studio, where it holds all manner of items used in the production of the soaps. Kim has a great eye, and the studio is filled with rustic baskets and other items for displaying her soaps when she takes them to markets.

Such a beautiful and important piece of furniture seems incongruous in a shed. It is attributed to George Thwaites and sons, a firm of cabinet-makers from Melbourne who made a great deal of the Victorian colony's earliest fine furniture, and dates from c. 1850–60. The design is simple but refined. The dresser may have started life as a bookcase – the shelf fronts look as if they have had scalloped leather panels below them at some stage, there are no drawers, and the cupboards can only be opened with a key. It must have seen some interesting times in the early days of frontier-city Melbourne.

Kim has a number of pieces by George Thwaites and sons in her home and all display the outstanding workmanship of the dresser. The cedar positively glows in the daylight that spills into the dark shed when the door is opened. A fine collection of decoy ducks sits on the top shelf, and the other shelves contain a superb collection of large and small mortars and pestles and birds' nests.

OPPOSITE
*Australian cedar dresser,*
*c. 1850–60*

# A PAINTER'S DRESSER

## MORGAN ALLENDER

A rose-covered stone cottage built by early settlers in the Adelaide Hills houses this dresser and its owners, Morgan Allender and her partner, furniture maker Justin Hermes. The dresser was built for Morgan's mother in the 1970s by a local craftsman and Morgan grew up with it.

When her mother gave it to her, Morgan decided to give it a makeover. She took the handles off and started to paint it, and then about halfway through painting she decided she liked the two-tone look and stopped there. So the cupboard base and the backing boards on the plate rack have been painted, and the rest has been left as it was, giving a nice balance between painted and unpainted timber. The dresser has clean lines without its handles, and looks surprisingly modern.

Morgan is a painter who produces moody large-scale canvases that are a cross between landscape and still life. She uses light and space in her art to convey mood and feeling. Her dresser reflects the same calm colour palette of mostly neutral tones and feels very individual, like her paintings.

Morgan displays ceramics and pottery by friends on her dresser, along with gifts, flea-market finds brought back from Europe, and vintage pieces. The jugs and the rows and stacks of bowls, plates and platters have been arranged with an artist's eye such that the dresser has become a huge still life in the dining room.

A single Julia's Rose sits on the dresser, and a simple glass vase of roses picked from the dreamy garden sits on the dining table made by Justin, whose work is just as calm in feeling and as pared back as the dresser.

OPPOSITE
*Handcrafted dresser, 1970s*

# MAGGIE AND COLIN'S BAROSSA DRESSER

## MAGGIE AND COLIN BEER

This big Barossa dresser from the 1850s or 1860s sits in the warm and inviting Barossa Valley kitchen of Maggie and Colin Beer. Maggie is a beloved Australian cook, author and television star, and Colin is a grape grower and pheasant farmer. They live in an early-colonial Barossa house, which is why the quite simple dresser looks so at home here – it was built to go into a house just like this. Three shelves hold a huge assortment of plates and objects, and a wide base holds lots more. The bottom section has two cupboards with two pointy shield panels on each door; the cupboards provide masses of storage for plates and large platters.

Over the years I have been lucky enough to visit Maggie and Colin's home many times, and it is always full of people and food, laughter and song. Every time I am there, I stand and look at the dresser's wonderful display of heirlooms, mementos, souvenirs of travel, props used in cookbook shoots, and photographs. Precious gifts from friends and items bought on overseas adventures line the shelves and cover every available surface, with a rabbit-shaped terrine, china plates, Sicilian pottery, ceramic chooks and pheasants jostling for space. A row of baskets on the top await trips to the orchard and vegetable garden, ready to be filled with harvested produce.

The kitchen is said to be the heart of a home, and this kitchen definitely is. Maggie and Colin's dresser – a repository of family items and love – partly inspired this book.

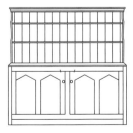

OPPOSITE
*Barossa Valley dresser,*
*c. 1850–60*

# DI'S DRESSER

This lovely pale-scrubbed-pine 1890s potboard dresser lives in a big country kitchen in central Victoria. Laden with china, copper, bowls, baskets and antique kitchen implements, it's the first thing you see when you walk into the room.

The dresser has good proportions, simple lines and no ornamentation. It looks as though it has always lived in the kitchen of this large Victorian home, but Di, the owner, bought it just a few years ago. She had been looking for the perfect dresser to replace one her husband had made while they waited for the right one. The dresser's plate rack originally had backing boards, but Di removed them to give the dresser a more open, airy feel. She has carefully stored the boards in case a future owner might wish to reinstate them.

The new dresser has settled in well. It has become home to some of Di's collection of kitchenalia and French china – plates, serving dishes, vegetable dishes, bowls, cups and a tureen – with vegetables painted on it. She uses the china every day. 'None of it is of much value or precious,' she says. 'It's just stuff that I love.' A pine corner cabinet with shelves holds the overflow of dishes and a lot more of the 'vegetable' china she collects.

Stacks of mixing bowls and baskets, copper jam pans and early kitchen devices fill the potboard of the dresser, and a locally made butter churn sits on the top with other kitchen treasures, including a maid's wooden bucket and a special potato basket. The antique English ceramic water filter came from a trip to Belgium and looks as if it has always been on the dresser. Di's favourite English meat dish is in the centre of the top shelf, and a favourite old lamp gives a warm glow at night.

As with a lot of dresser owners, Di stores cutlery in one of the two wide drawers and important bits and pieces in the other – balls of string, sticky tape and bits and bobs essential to daily life. A child's chair to the side holds some of her well-used cookbooks. This is the kitchen of a real country cook.

OPPOSITE
*Pine potboard dresser, c. 1890*

LEFT
Pine dresser, 19th century

RIGHT
Pine corner cabinet, 19th century

# RED
# CART
# VINTAGE

—

# KATHY
# O'NEILL

Some antique shops and vintage stores have a certain magic, a certain atmosphere, a certain feel. It's hard to put your finger on, but when you walk in the door you feel a rush of adrenaline and a palpable sense of excitement and anticipation: there are treasures waiting to be discovered!

These stores are few and far between, but when you find one, you need to keep going back. The collecting bug is like a drug, and shops like these know how to feed your habit. It's partly how the goods are displayed, but it's also the dealer's personality and eye, and the magic they create in the combinations of objects, the space, and the way the shop is lit.

Red Cart Vintage in the central Victorian town of Kyneton is one such shop. You never know what you will find there. On every visit you will see or buy a new treasure. Who knew you needed a taxidermy fox or Japanese glass fishing-net floats or a superb old dresser?

Kathy O'Neill, who calls herself a 'hunter and gatherer', is the person behind Red Cart Vintage. She has an eye for the unusual and understands how to make great displays of the strange and wonderful objects she sources and sells. The shop has a dedicated following, especially among people moving from the city to the country. They might be leaving a tiny apartment for a country house and looking for a dresser and other furniture for their new home.

Red Cart is a good place to find a dresser. Kathy says they usually have at least one or two in stock and often more waiting to be brought in. You might find a scrubbed-pine shield-door dresser, a painted Depression-era dresser made from old packing cases, or a dark Victorian dresser. Kathy displays vintage china, kitchenalia and other treasures on the dressers in the store – and, of course, those dressers are for sale as well.

OPPOSITE (LEFT DRESSER)
*Edwardian dresser,*
*early 20th century*

OPPOSITE (RIGHT DRESSER)
*Victorian pine dresser,*
*late 19th century*

# MOTHER-AND-SON DRESSER OWNERS

---

# MARDI SLOAN AND NICHOLAS SCOTT

Nicholas Scott and his mother, Mardi Sloan, are both owners of oak dressers. Mardi lives in the city in a chic apartment, while Nicholas lives in the country and grows flowers for florists on his property, Oak Farm. Each dresser reflects its owner and where they live.

Mardi's 18th-century oak dresser displays a stylish mix of family silver and china and, of course, flowers from Nicholas's country garden.

Nicholas's dresser always has flowers on it, too, along with an accumulation of lovely things – green Wedgwood cabbage-leaf plates, enamel boxes, pewter and special bits of china from his travels and from local flea markets. Royal-memorabilia tins, a vase of feathers and the odd bird's nest from the garden help fill the dresser.

Nicholas was the very happy winning bidder at the weekly auction of a Melbourne auction house, and his 18th-century English oak dresser feels like it's always been in the corner of his kitchen. It has five drawers with cockbeading. There is no potboard but it does have a beautiful arch that is a perfect spot for a dog bed.

If you look carefully, you can see a link between the two dressers: the teal-blue meat platter that sits at the top of Nicholas's dresser is part of the same dinner service that fills the shelves of Mardi's dresser.

Pip, Nicholas's trusty companion, is at home in both the city and the country. When you visit Oak Farm you will often find her asleep in her bed under the arch of Nicholas's dresser.

OPPOSITE
*Oak dresser, 18th century*

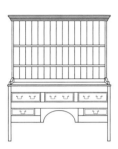

English oak dresser,
18th century

# A CABINET OF CURIOSITIES

## PETER COOPER AND KAREN HALL

A 19th-century child's boot made from reindeer hide – purchased during a trip to Lapland – is one of the sculptural objects that fill Peter Cooper and Karen Hall's dresser. There are no china or ceramic items on this dresser, which is instead used as a cabinet of curiosities, a place to store mementos of travel.

The dresser sits on turned feet, which means it doesn't feel too heavy or dominant in the couple's sitting room. It has seven drawers and an inset cupboard in the middle of the base, all with turned wooden knobs. It was sold to Peter and Karen as a Welsh pine dresser and is a particularly attractive colour; it probably dates from the late 18th century and may have been painted at some stage, as there is the odd tiny trace of paint. The plate rack has three shelves, very wide backing boards, and beautifully shaped supports at the sides. A pot of devil's ivy adds to the display, the green leaves contrasting nicely with the pale pine.

Every object on the dresser tells a story of a holiday, a journey or an adventure the couple have had together. A wooden box with a handle and a row of iron teeth is a blueberry picker from northern Scandinavia, and items from Lapland and Asia, including the islands of Indonesia, line the shelves alongside family photographs, batik printing blocks and old books. The dresser has only been with the couple for seven years, but it has settled into their home and looks like it rather enjoys its position as keeper of their *aide-mémoires*.

OPPOSITE
*Welsh pine dresser,
late 18th century*

# A TASMANIAN DRESSER

---

## PENNY DUNN

This elegant Huon pine dresser of beautiful proportions and colour belongs to Penny Dunn. Its simple lines fit well with her china and her Georgian furniture. She bought it in the 1980s from a dealer in Kyncton, Victoria, and it has lived in many homes with her over the years.

The dresser must have started out life in Tasmania in the 1860s, as it has a typical Tasmanian frieze at the top of the plate rack. The backing boards are quite wide, and the simplicity of the single drawer with a turned knob and the table-like base add to its elegance. A stack of meat platters sits in the middle of the potboard, and a beautifully curated and balanced display of Penny's favourite pieces fills the shelves. Six French oyster plates with oyster-shaped depressions live happily alongside the collection of Spode pieces with 'Chelsea' and 'Chinese Rose' patterns. A couple of contemporary ceramic pieces and some pewter add to the mix.

Penny makes lovely marmalade, and a few jars wait on the dresser top to be given to friends. Two tall lamps with turned bases and card shades complete the look, and their light adds atmosphere to the dining area in the evening.

OPPOSITE
*Tasmanian Huon pine dresser,
c. 1860*

# COLONIAL
SURVIVORS

—

## SHARON
RANDALL

This early-colonial Australian 'primitive' dresser with shield cupboard doors belongs to Sharon Randall, a collector and dealer in vintage and antique Christmas decorations. It dates from before 1900 and came from the clearing sale of an old house in Kyneton. Before that, its original home was in Chiltern in north-eastern Victoria. Sharon's husband, Ron, is from that area of Victoria, so Sharon took that as a sign that it was meant for them. They have had it for eighteen years and it has travelled to various homes with them.

The dresser has its original paint finish, which has developed into fine crazed patina from years of hot Australian summers. The dark finish is quite striking and unusual, and gives the dresser an almost modern look.

What does a vintage Christmas ornament collector decorate her dresser with? Antique and vintage ornaments, of course! The dresser and its shelves have become a tableau of Sharon's extensive collection of early Christmas decorations, old china, tin jelly moulds and wooden butter stamps. A small forest of bottlebrush Christmas trees from the United States has sprung up, populated by a family of 1920s stick-leg sheep under the watchful gaze of a mountain goat, reindeer and chamois-covered cows. The colour palette is carefully controlled to warm browns and variations of white and cream.

Sharon has another dresser, bought from Red Cart Vintage (see page 193), that holds part of her kitchenalia collection. This rustic homemade piece of unknown age came from a farmhouse in the Pyrenees area of western Victoria and has its original grey paint. Many primitive early dressers, like this one, were made from whatever bits and pieces were at hand: recycled timber, sometimes old packing cases. These lucky survivors of Australia's colonial past would have been used in shearers' accommodation and farm labourers' cottages.

OPPOSITE
*Australian colonial dresser, pre-1900*

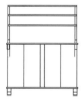

FOLLOWING (RIGHT)
*Rustic handmade dresser, late 19th century*

# THE
DRESSER
AT
WOOMARGAMA

---

## THE
DARLING
FAMILY

A jug full of garden-grown roses sits on the dresser in the dining room at Woomargama, the farm owned by the late Margaret Darling.

This is a pared-back English oak and elm table dresser, with three generous drawers and four shelves on the plate rack to display china. Simple but elegant tapered legs and no potboard give it a lighter feel so that it doesn't dominate the space, as a more solid dresser would. The only embellishments are the wonderful scrolled bracket supports at the ends of the dresser top.

Margaret had a collection of early English china and 18th-century teapots. Shown here is a stunning c. 1820s Coalport tea set that sings quietly against the wide-planked backboard of the dresser in simple and understated style, just like the farmhouse and its late owner.

OPPOSITE
*English oak and elm dresser,*
*18th century*

# A COLOURFUL HARVEST

## SOPHIE THOMSON

Sophie Thomson lives in a very old early-colonial stone cottage in the Adelaide Hills surrounded by a productive garden full of fruit trees, vegetables and herbs – as well as kids and animals. You might know her as one of the presenters on ABC TV's *Gardening Australia*.

Sophie's large 19th-century scrubbed-pine dresser was probably made in Australia. It lives in the cottage kitchen and she has been collecting for years to fill it. What does a mad-keen gardener and vegetable grower put on her dresser? Ceramic fruit and vegetables, of course! These take the form of dishes, plates, bowls, jugs, teapots and salt and pepper shakers, with the odd ceramic caterpillar and bird to keep the harvest company.

The display is colourful and original: there are no regimented ranks of blue-and-white plates here. Many different ceramicists are represented – some Australian, some not – but the pieces sit happily together in this show of plenty. The table in front of the dresser holds platters and bowls of fresh produce from the garden. There's a sense of generosity and family in this home, and the dresser and its vibrant contents are at the very centre.

OPPOSITE
*Australian pine dresser,
19th century*

# THE DRESSER AT RUNNYMEDE HOUSE

## NATIONAL TRUST OF AUSTRALIA (TASMANIA)

The Huon pine dresser at Runnymede House in Hobart sits gently glowing in the kitchen, filled with period china and jelly moulds. On the polished top is a bowl of walnuts from the tree in the garden. Opposite, the kitchen table is set with paraphernalia of the time, and an 1840s cookbook is open at a recipe – perhaps it's what the owner of the house is having for dinner. It's as if the cook has just stepped out for a moment.

This Hobart-made dresser, c. 1840, sits against a white wall on the original flagstones. It has a beautifully shaped frieze at the top, and the backing boards are alternately narrow and wide. There are three shelves with stepped shape supports at the ends. The top of the dresser is a single piece of Huon pine and under that are three drawers with turned blackwood knobs that have been ebonised. Below the drawers are four cupboards.

Runnymede House is a National Trust property that originally belonged to a whaling captain, Captain Charles Bayley. You can sense the presence of past occupants in its rooms and in pieces like this dresser, which were part of life in colonial times.

OPPOSITE
*Huon pine dresser, c. 1840*

# THE MAYFIELD DRESSER

---

## TRACEY HAYNES

Tracey Haynes describes her dresser as the heart of her home and where everything happens. It holds some of her vast collection of Emma Bridgewater china, which she started collecting when she was living in England, plus children's toys, artworks, model planes and even a vintage cap gun. At one end is the drinks department. Tracey's kids have taken over one of the drawers and it's full of coloured pencils, crayons and felt-tip pens.

The modern painted dresser started life as a shop fitting in a country provisions store. Tracey says it was a serendipitous find – she walked into the store a few years ago when it was going out of business, and the dresser was one of the last things left. She and her husband, Richard, were renovating Mayfield, their home in central Victoria, and she needed somewhere to store things while the renovations happened.

The dresser is quite large with very deep shelves that are perfect for holding masses of china. Kids' sports ribbons line the top shelf and artworks decorate the front. The wide shelves are far more practical than standard shelves: whole dinner sets fit into each alcove but still display the china beautifully. Baskets on the potboard contain items that need to be stored and not seen. Tracey must have the biggest collection of Emma Bridgewater china in Australia. A rather large Georgian housekeeper's cupboard in the dining room holds more of this collection and keeps everything close at hand.

Even though it's tall and imposing, the dresser is the perfect scale for Tracey's sizeable country kitchen. She isn't keen on fitted kitchens, so she has blue-and-white striped skirts rather than cupboard doors. A gorgeous cream Aga oven set into a tiled alcove keeps the kitchen the warmest room in the house in winter.

This is a proper country farmhouse kitchen and Tracey is a skilled cook. If you drop in to visit, she will quickly bake a batch of perfect scones in the Aga and serve a big pot of tea using a teapot and mugs from the dresser.

OPPOSITE
*Painted hardwood dresser,
21st century*

# THE DRESSER AT TICKLETANK

## IRENE PEARCE

In 1998 Irene Pearce bought an old 50,000-gallon concrete tank in the Adelaide Hills and turned it into a light-filled home – quite a feat considering the tank had water in it when she purchased it! The home is called Tickletank and Irene says people are tickled pink when they see it.

On a postage stamp of land (450 square metres) in Mount Barker, she created a now-famous whimsical garden around the tank from scratch. Irene opens her garden every year, and it's been featured many times on television and in gardening magazines.

Irene can do just about anything. She is a potter and sculptor by trade but can turn her hand to building, gardening and cooking (she bakes fantastic scones), creating a magical environment for herself. On entering the tank you are struck by how much of her furniture is built in and wonder why there aren't more houses like it. It's a brilliant way to live. Irene made most of the furniture, largely from salvaged materials. Her artist's eye is able to see the possibilities in bits and pieces she gets for almost nothing.

The dresser is constructed of concrete blocks, rendered and then painted white, and odds and ends from various sources. The upper glazed cupboard doors and the row of small drawers came from another piece of furniture, as did the lower cupboard doors. The top is a mosaic of broken white tiles, and the drawers and upper cupboard doors have been given a crackle-glaze finish. The whole thing is painted a crisp white and acts as a great foil for Irene's colourful collection of pottery and ceramics and vases of greenery from the garden. The dresser functions well and stores masses of stuff. Irene keeps some of her mother's china in the upper cupboard, as she likes to see and enjoy it rather than have it tucked away out of sight.

The whole house is bright, warm and inviting – vastly different from the dark water tank Irene bought years ago. It feels like a house on a Greek island rather than one in the Adelaide Hills.

OPPOSITE
*Dresser made from rendered concrete blocks and salvaged timber items, 20th century*

# THE INTERIOR DESIGNER'S DRESSER

## CARLOS SÁNCHEZ-GARCÍA

Set in the beauty of the Norfolk countryside in England is the farmhouse of interior designer Carlos Sánchez-García and his husband, Michael. Two contented whippets – Tristan and Theodora – bask next to the Aga in the warm and inviting country kitchen.

Set in the heart of the kitchen is Carlos's very fine 17th-century Welsh oak canopy dresser. The proportions are perfect and it's all original except for the 18th-century handles. It has subtle details: for example, the reeding that is normally carved on the doors and drawers of a dresser is carved on the body of this piece.

The dresser's dark patina makes it perfect for displaying a colourful array of pottery, plates and figures, mostly from the 19th century, to their best advantage. The big central piece on the top shelf, a Prince of Wales Staffordshire figure on horseback in glorious peach and green colours, is a favourite of Carlos's. It is flanked by a set of Scottish spongeware bowls and two Sunderland lustreware cream jugs. The middle shelf holds a collection of 19th-century Eastern European bowls of different colours and sizes, while the bottom shelf features a trio of colourful Staffordshire hens, a pair of Victorian pearlware candlesticks and some Gaudy Welsh jugs and mugs. The shelves also hold invitations and thank-you cards. A lamp with an ikat shade gives the dresser, and indeed the kitchen, atmosphere at night.

Opposite the oak dresser is a glazed pine dresser from the start of the 20th century. It contains glassware that is used every day, some large pearlware bowls and, on the lower shelves, Spanish blue-and-white bowls; the pearlware and blue-and-white bowls were given to Carlos by his grandmother.

Carlos often uses dressers in his interior designs. He says, 'They are not only beautiful but extremely useful pieces of furniture and allow the client to bring their personality into the design by highlighting their special or everyday wares.'

OPPOSITE
*Detail of Welsh oak canopy dresser, 17th century*

OPPOSITE
*Pine dresser with glazed doors,
early 20th century*

# TALL
# AND
# NARROW

---

## VINCENT
## JENDEN

This unusual dresser lives in the country home of designer Vincent Jenden and his partner, Robert. The tall, narrow black-painted dresser with a fretwork gallery on top, three drawers and a cupboard takes up very little room but adds quite a bit of storage, considering how small it is.

Vincent bought it from the weekly auction at a Melbourne auction house and thinks it was probably put together from bits and pieces of other furniture as a 'marriage piece', or was perhaps designed to hold books. Either way, it works perfectly in his kitchen and proves that dressers don't need to be huge and take up lots of room. This type of dresser would also work well in a city apartment or a tiny cottage.

The dresser is filled with green items: crockery, vases, cabbage-ware plates, glass, a tin of favourite tea, and some well-placed books. It sits between two black-painted chairs upholstered in acid-green fabric that continue the theme – Vincent loves green. It pops against the stripped lining board walls of the country house and adds a touch of drama and colour to the kitchen.

OPPOSITE
*Painted timber dresser,
20th century*

# THE COLLECTORS

*Dresser made from a*
*repurposed oak chest and*
*plate rack, c. 18th century*

FOLLOWING (LEFT)
*Hardwood dresser with crusty*
*original patinated paint, 1920s*

FOLLOWING (RIGHT)
*Corner bookcase given new life*
*as a dresser, 19th century*

Walking into Michele and her partner Phil's house, you immediately know you are in the home of real collectors. An early-colonial Australian cedar Barossa dresser, c. 1840s, filled with decoy ducks greets you in the entrance hall and gives you a taste of the collections within the house.

Michele's collections are many and varied: taxidermy, carved breadboards, decoy ducks, manikins, kitchenalia, spongeware, Bosley bread crocks, tureens and dressers. She has not one but six dressers, as well as a corner cabinet that is set up as a dresser. Everywhere you look, arrangements of objects delight the eye. Every table and every corner contain beautiful things. Michele takes great pleasure in changing the displays, so each time you visit things will have moved around.

When you go into the main living area, the first thing you see is Michele's 18th-century Irish pine dresser with a gorgeous arrangement of spongeware bowls and a double row of dark-green French and English majolica plates. A taxidermy South African klipspringer and two Bosley Pottery bread crocks complete the display.

In an alcove off the main room, two painted Australian dressers of unknown age face each other with a table and chairs between them. The arrangements on these two dressers are no less stunning than the one on the Irish pine dresser. A collection of spongeware ceramics and another two Bosley Pottery bread crocks live on the dark painted dresser, and a joyous colourful collection of majolica and ceramics occupy the cream painted dresser opposite. There is so much to take in on this dresser. A majolica cheese dome forms the centre of the arrangement and two brown Bargeware teapots sit on either side with their decorative mini-teapot finials.

An oak mule chest (probably 18th century) in another part of the house has been converted to a dresser a long time ago, with the addition of a slightly later plate rack, and doors that create cupboards on the base rather than a hinged lid. This dresser is home to part of Michele's collection of carved breadboards and butter stamps, and the warm glow of the polished wood contrasts with the dark oak. An English slipware dairy bowl and a butter churn add to the display.

In the sitting room, a 19th-century glazed corner cabinet has been pressed into duty as a mini dresser and is filled with china, ceramic jelly moulds, Staffordshire dogs and a fascinating model of toadstools. Another dresser in this room – a local auction find, with simple lines – holds cutlery trays, wooden bowls and antique rag balls.

*Australian cedar and pine dresser, c. 1940s*

*Barossa Valley cedar dresser, 1880s or earlier*

Irish pine dresser, 18th century

251

# ACKNOWLEDGEMENTS

Thanks to Kirsten Abbott, publisher extraordinaire, and her team at Thames & Hudson Australia; Katie Purvis for editing my words; Ashlea O'Neill for her wonderful design and for understanding the project; and Tim Bowen for agreeing to write the foreword – Diolch yn fawr.

A big thank you to all the dresser owners who allowed me to include their beautiful dressers in the book:

Mum and Dad
Alison Hawkes
Allan Davis
Anna
Biankah Miller:
 instagram.com/thecollektive
Carlos Sánchez-García:
 carlosgarciainteriors.com
Carolyn Imlach at the Evandale Village Store:
 thevillage.store
Chelly and Peter Gray:
 shadesofgray.net.au
Christine Reid
Cornelius Horgan
Daniel Burgermeister
The Darling family
Debbie and Cameron Wilson at the Jardin Room:
 thejardinroom.com.au
Di
Florida and Miles Rickard-Kerr
Glenny Eastwood
Harvey and Carol Wilkins at Westbury Antiques:
 westburyantiques.com.au
Irene Pearce
James Broadbent
Janet Niven
Kathy O'Neill at Red Cart Vintage:
 red-cart-vintage.business.site
Kaye Pickett
Kelly Mott
Kim Rowlatt
Maggie and Colin Beer
Mardi Sloan

May Petschel
Michael Dale
Michael McWilliam and Robert Henley
Michele and Phil
Michelle Hylan and Cliff Pannam
Morgan Allender:
 morganallender.com
Natasha Alvey
Neil Robertson
Nexus Designs:
 nexusdesigns.com.au
Ngaire and Roger Hudson
Nicholas Scott
Penny Dunn
Peter Cooper and Karen Hall
Peter Woof at Evandale Antiques:
 6A Russell Street, Evandale, Tasmania
Runnymede House:
 nationaltrust.org.au/places/runnymede
Ryn England at Whisk and Wheelbarrow:
 instagram.com/whiskandwheelbarrow
Sharon Randall
Sophie Thomson
Tara Badcock:
 instagram.com/tarabadcockartist
Tracey Haynes
Val Hawkes
Vincent Jenden:
 vincentjenden.com/profile

And a huge thankyou to Warwick Oakman for all the leads to Tasmanian dressers:
 warwickoakman.com

# BIBLIOGRAPHY

Bebb, Richard, *Welsh Furniture 1250–1950: A Cultural History of Craftsmanship and Design* (2 vols), Saer Books, Kidwelly, 2007.

Bowen, Tim & Betsan Bowen, *The Welsh Stick Chair: A Visual Record*, Pethe Press, 2020.

Davies, T Alun, *The Welsh Dresser and Associated Cupboards*, University of Wales Press & National Museum of Wales, Cardiff, 1991.

Pennell, Sara, *The Birth of the English Kitchen, 1600–1850*, Bloomsbury Academic, London, 2017.

Rendell, Jane, 'The Welsh Dresser: An Atlas', in Brandon LaBelle (ed.), *Surface Tension: Problematics of Site*, Errant Bodies Press, Los Angeles, 2003.

Stephens, Chris S & Eleri Davies, *The Welsh Dresser*, Gomer Press, Llandysul, 2013.

Vincentelli, Moira, *Women and Ceramics: Gendered Vessels*, Manchester University Press, Manchester, 2000.

Watkins, Flora, 'The Kitchen Dresser, and Why It's More Important than Central Heating', *Country Life*, 21 June 2017.

First published in Australia in 2022
by Thames & Hudson Australia Pty Ltd
11 Central Boulevard, Portside Business Park
Port Melbourne, Victoria 3207
ABN: 72 004 751 964

First published in the United Kingdom in 2022
by Thames & Hudson Ltd
181a High Holborn
London WC1V 7QX

Thames & Hudson Australia wishes to
acknowledge that Aboriginal and Torres Strait
Islander people are the first storytellers of this
nation and the traditional custodians of the land
on which we live and work. We acknowledge their
continuing culture and pay respect to Elders past,
present and future.

ISBN 978-1-760-76103-5

A catalogue record for this
book is available from the
National Library of Australia

British Library Cataloguing-in-Publication Data
A catalogue record for this book is available from
the British Library

Front cover: Christine Reid's Welsh oak high
dresser, c. 1760

Design: Ashlea O'Neill | Salt Camp Studio
Illustration: Ashlea O'Neill | Salt Camp Studio
Editing: Katie Purvis
Printed and bound in China by 1010 Printing
International Limited

FSC® is dedicated to the promotion of responsible
forest management worldwide. This book is made
of material from FSC®-certified forests and other
controlled sources.

Be the first to know about our new releases,
exclusive content and author events by visiting
**thamesandhudson.com.au**
**thamesandhudson.com**
**thamesandhudsonusa.com**

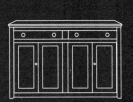
Early-colonial painted and distressed dresser, c. 1825

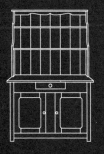
Huon pine dresser, late 19th century

Oak dresser, c. 1760–70

Oak George III high dresser with mahogany cross-banded drawers, from Lancashire, c. 1760

Welsh cwpwrdd deuddarn from Snowdonia, 1769

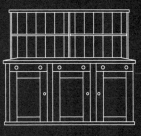
Tasmanian pine dresser, 19th century

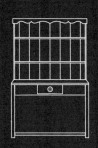
Tasmanian Huon pine dresser, 19th century

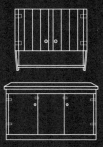
Australian dresser, homemade from reclaimed timber, 20th century

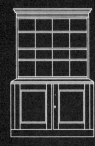
Australian cedar dresser, c. 1850–60

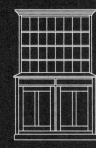
Handcrafted dresser, 1970s

Victorian pine dresser, late 19th century

Oak dresser, 18th century

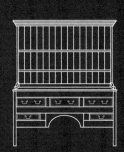
English oak dresser, 18th century

Welsh pine dresser, late 18th century

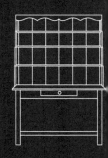
Tasmanian Huon pine dresser, c. 1860

Painted hardwood dresser, 21st century

Dresser made from rendered concrete blocks and salvaged timber items, 20th century

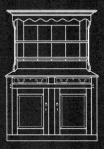
Welsh oak canopy dresser, 17th century

Pine dresser with glazed doors, early 20th century

Painted timber dresser, 20th century